My Past Lovers

Poems of Love and Loss

Regina Elaine Romandetti

BookLeaf
Publishing

India | USA | UK

Made with ❤ on the BookLeaf Publishing Platform
www.bookleafpub.in
www.bookleafpub.com

Dedication

This book is dedicated to all the men I've had the privilege of loving at some point in my life.

Preface

This book is a journey through love, pain, and growth. A reflection on the men who have been a part of my life and the lessons they've left behind.

Acknowledgements

I want to thank my family and friends, who have always let me dream freely and supported me no matter what life has brought my way.

My First Love

My first love.
On the first day of middle school,
you called me the wrong name just to get my attention—
and the rest was history.
We'd get ourselves into trouble, sometimes skipping
class.
We were always laughing.
We used to meet up to go ice skating, convinced we were
the best.
You taught me how to drive, and we'd talk about the
future.
If it wasn't for you, I would've never gone to college.
You said we were going to get married—you'd become a
police officer, and I'd be a teacher.
I kept up my end of the bargain.
You're living your best life now,
and it's been years since we last saw each other.
I always find myself wondering
What if life had happened the way we had planned?

Christopher

I hate that we had so much more to say,
Now, I won't get that chance.
Our timing was off.
They say, "Right person, wrong time,"
And that seems to happen a lot.
I used to call you an old man with a smile on my face,
But you were too young for what had happened.
It wasn't fair.
I hate that the memories we made together
Are ones I have no one to share with.
I hate that I had to know what it's like to lose you.
We were so much more to each other than what we
allowed.
Stubbornness and stupidity—that's what we were.
I hate that I think of you every damn day.
You'll never know how mad I am at you
For leaving so soon without saying a goodbye.

26

I would cry at my mother's bedroom door,
Begging her, "Does life get any better?"
Asking, "How can I spend the rest of my days
Feeling so empty and hopeless?"
And my mother would answer softly,
"You're only 26."

Let me Go

We would scream at each other,
Begging each other to stay—
But in different ways.
I wanted more,
& you didn't.
You wouldn't let me go.
And I didn't want to leave.
I cried and yelled,
"Please, let me go."

One to Many

When we first met, you were a gentleman.
You picked me up for our first date.
Took me to dinner, paid.
Had just one drink.
I was comfortable.

Everything seemed perfect—
You introduced me to your friends and family,
It all felt right.

Then you got comfortable.
One drink turned into too many—too many to count.
Your words began to slur, and they weren't so nice
anymore.
Your friends hated me, blamed me.
I was uncomfortable.

Space.

I don't know how to give space; it's all or nothing.

Dress

Every time you picked me up in your car,
You'd tell me to wear something sexy.
I would oblige, slipping into a dress,
Scooting into the passenger seat,
Your hand creeping up my thigh.
You'd ask to see what was underneath
And though I cringed, I would agree
Not wanting to disappoint you,
Yet all along,
I was disappointing myself.

Time and Place

Soft-spoken, kind, respectful, and well-mannered
outside,
How is it that once we are inside,
A switch goes off behind closed doors?
With a twinkle in your eye,
You become rough and tough, throwing me across the
sheets—
Always a gentleman who knows the time and place.

Handsome Face

You're a dad, but not mine,
Telling me to *do this and that,*
What to do, how to do it, how to move.
Put it there, now move around.
And all I can say is, *okay,*
To your handsome face.

Pasta

How is it that when I'm all worked up
With anger and stress,
You walk through the door,
Calm me down,
And all you have to say is,
"Baby, it will all be alright."

You're soothing and comforting,
Like a warm bowl of pasta on a Sunday

Voodoo

Italian Voodoo.

Did I believe in it? Never—until I met you.

On paper, we are perfect.

Brown eyes, brown hair, traditional.

Catholic education, classic.

Manners and politeness—our mothers raised us well.

Strong-minded, headstrong.

It's almost like someone cast a spell to pull us together.

Letters

You knew how to BS,
But I had earned a BS.
Once, you told me
"You're too pretty to be so stupid."
You, with a GED.
Thanks for pushing me to finish *my* MA,
And soon, I'll chase a PhD.
It's all letters, for sure.
But now they spell me free away from you.

All the days....

It's simple.
I love your face,
Your nose, your lips,
And all the things
I cannot share.
You are you,
And I am me.
I love you all the days.

Cut me off

You cut me off
And took my parking spot.
Then you sat behind me in class.
When the professor asked,
"Who wants to be partners for the semester?"
You grabbed my arm,
Raised it high,
And said,
"We would be"

We were a whirlwind—
Young and wild.
Anytime I think of you,
I happen to always smile.

Family

The hardest part of breakups
Is losing their family, too.
I still think of his mom,
Who made the best Mofongo,
Or his dad,
Who I once called mine,
Both treating me like a daughter.
And his little brother—
He could've been my own.
Even though I'm no longer
A part of their world,
I will keep them in my heart forever.

Keeping the best parts.

Why can't I keep all the best parts
Of everyone I've ever loved?
I'd take one's eyes,
Another's family,
That one's smile,
And one's calming aura.
The one who protected me,
The one who stood beside me
And definitely the one who was the life of the party.
I'd gather all the best parts.
I know it's not possible,
But it's fun to imagine how you can create the perfect
man.

The world.

From the outside,
We looked like we had nothing in common
But in our bubble,
We were perfect.
Lost in love,
We laughed,
We dreamed,
We talked about life.
We learned from each other.
It felt like we had it all together.

Out of nowhere you broke my heart.
You said you loved me,
But knew you couldn't give me the world.

Tattoo

They say tattoos are only skin deep,
But I'm certain his went straight to my heart.

I refer to as my ex.

When I talk about you, I refer to you as my ex.
Maybe because, deep down, I really wanted to be able to
call you mine.
We weren't together in the traditional sense—
I can count on one hand how many times I saw your
face.
But whenever I was in trouble, you were the first person
I called.
You knew my secrets, and I knew yours.
You cared, even if you wouldn't admit it.
You were too busy, always focused on your plan—a plan
I knew I was never really part of,
though I would always pretend I was.

Name

You call me baby, beautiful, and sexy—like those are my
name.
You don't see my roots growing out or the ten pounds
I've gained.
You don't notice how tired I am from work, chasing
deadlines, and meeting life's demands.
You say I'm perfect—and somehow, that's all I need.

In the morning

In the morning, while brushing my teeth,
I used to tell myself I was beautiful,
I was strong,
and I could do anything.
I didn't need anyone.
Then I met you, and you took that place—
you filled me up with those kind words.
But when you left, I forgot how to fill myself up again.